Carpenters
Community Workers

by Vicky Franchino

Content Adviser: Dennis Day,
Associated General Contractors of America

Reading Adviser: Dr. Linda D. Labbo,
Department of Reading Education, College of Education,
The University of Georgia

COMPASS POINT BOOKS

Minneapolis, Minnesota

Compass Point Books
3722 West 50th Street, #115
Minneapolis, MN 55410

Visit Compass Point Books on the Internet at *www.compasspointbooks.com* or e-mail your
request to *custserv@compasspointbooks.com*

Photographs ©:
Photo Network/Steve Agricola; cover, Visuals Unlimited/Jeff Greenberg; 4; 5 right, Mark Skalny, 5, Index Stock Imagery; 6,
International Stock/Westerman; 7, FPG International/Gary Buss; 8, Index Stock /Eric Kamp; 9, FPG International/Telegraph Colour
Library; 10, FPG International/Gary Buss; 11, International Stock /Phyllis Picardi; 12, FPG International/Ron Chapple; 13, FPG
International/Stephen Simpson; 14, International Stock/Patrick Ramsey; 15, Photo Network/D. and I. MacDonald; 16, Visuals
Unlimited/ Nancy P. Alexander; 17, Visuals Unlimited/Mark E. Gibson; 18, David F. Clobes; 19, Visuals Unlimited/ Peter Holden;
20, Visuals Unlimited/Jeff Greenberg; 21, International Stock/Elliot Smith; 22, Photo Network/Tom Campbell; 23, Unicorn Stock
Photos/Mike Morris; 24, Unicorn Stock Photos/Jeff Greenberg; 25, FPG International/Arthur Tilley; 26, Index Stock Imagery; 27

Editors: E. Russell Primm and Emily J. Dolbear
Photo Researcher: Svetlana Zhurkina
Photo Selector: Linda S. Koutris
Design: Bradfordesign, Inc.

Library of Congress Cataloging-in-Publication Data

Franchino, Vicky.
    Carpenters / by Vicky Franchino.
        p. cm. — (Community workers)
    Includes bibliographical references and index.
    Summary: Briefly describes different types of carpenters and the various projects they help complete.
    ISBN 0-7565-0006-0
        1. Carpenters—Juvenile literature. [1. Carpenters. 2. Occupations.] I. Title. II. Series.
    TH5608.7 .F725 2000
    694'.023—dc21   00-008618

Table of Contents

What Do Carpenters Do?

Carpenters use wood to build things. They build houses and stores. Clocks and furniture. Treehouses and skyscrapers. Carpenters build many unusual things too. They build sets for TV shows and rides for theme parks.

A carpenter makes furniture.

An apprentice carpenter works on a boat.

What Tools and Equipment Do They Use?

Carpenters need many tools to do their job. Power tools need electricity but hand tools do not. Some hand tools have not changed much over time.

◀ A carpenter's hand tools

A carpenter uses a power saw. ▶

Measuring tools help carpenters lay out and measure the wood. They use saws to cut wood and drills to make holes. Hammers and screwdrivers help them put the pieces of wood together. They use a tool called a **level** to make sure that their work is perfectly straight.

◀ A carpenter using a power drill

A level ▶

How Do Carpenters Help?

Carpenters make buildings safe and strong. They build many things people need. They make beautiful things, such as furniture and clocks. They also keep buildings in good shape and fix things that are broken.

◀ A carpenter in his workshop

A carpenter ▶ remodels a house.

Where Do They Work?

Some carpenters work outside—even when it is very cold or very hot! Some carpenters do the inside work that will be seen once the job is done. Everything they do must look good.

◄ A carpenter installs a floor.

Measuring a ► wall stud

Who Do They Work With?

Carpenters work mostly with other carpenters and the **contractor**. The contractor is the person in charge of a building project. Carpenters also work with **architects**. Architects design buildings.

Contractors reviewing plans

An architect telephones her client while reviewing plans.

What Do They Wear?

Safety is important to all carpenters. Carpenters wear safety glasses to protect their eyes and special head-phones to cover their ears. Carpenters on a **construction site** wear hard hats and gloves.

◄ A carpenter wears safety glasses when he uses a power saw.

Carpenters wearing ► hard hats, safety glasses, and gloves

What Training Does It Take?

If you want to be a carpenter, you can start as a carpenter's helper. This means that you learn on the job from a skilled carpenter. Or you can become an **apprentice**. Apprentices take classes in school and also work at a construction site. Then, you become a **journeyman**—even if you are a woman!

Building the frame for a wall

A carpenter uses a tool to make corners, called a miter.

What Skills Do They Need?

Carpenters must know math and know how to measure things. They often say, "Measure twice, cut once." When carpenters measure twice before they cut, they don't make as many mistakes. This saves time as well as wood.

Carpenters must also understand **geometry**—a special kind of math that deals with circles, squares, and angles.

◄ Measuring wood

Using a carpenter's square ▶
to measure angles

What Problems Do They Face?

Construction carpenters must be strong and healthy. Sometimes they have to lift heavy pieces of wood. And they stand on their feet most of the day, which is very tiring. They also may work high in the air or deep in the ground. It's easy to see why carpenters can't be afraid of high places or low spaces.

◀ Sometimes carpenters have to work high in the air.

Carpenters build ▶ the frame for a house.

Would You Like to Be a Carpenter?

Do you like making things? Do you like working with your hands? Maybe you would like to be a carpenter someday. You can prepare now. Look for classes in carpentry. Offer to help family members who like to build things.

A young carpenter learns to use a power tool.

These students learn carpentry in school.

A Carpenter's Tools and Clothes

hard hat

level

tool belt

gloves

At the Construction Site

roof

frame

support beam

wall panel

base floor

A Carpenter's Day

Early morning
- A carpenter arrives at work just after sunrise.
- First, she talks to the contractor about what has to be done today.
- Then, she looks at the plans and lays out the work with the other carpenters.

Noon
- After measuring the wood twice, she cuts it with a saw.
- Then, she nails and glues the pieces together.
- Lunchtime! The carpenters eat their lunch outside. They will eat in a truck if it is raining.

Afternoon
- The carpenter finishes the wooden frames that support the walls.
- Once the frame is up, the carpenters put in the base flooring and wall panels.

Evening
- The carpenter puts her hand and power tools in order.
- Late in the afternoon, she leaves the work site.
- During the busy building season, she may work seven days a week.

Night
- The carpenter goes to bed early. Tomorrow, she heads to a new work site!

Glossary

apprentice—a person who works for a skilled carpenter in order to learn

architects—people who design buildings

construction site—the place where a building is being built

contractor—the person in charge of a building project

geometry—a special kind of math that deals with circles, squares, and angles

journeyman—someone who worked as an apprentice and learned a trade

level—a tool used to make sure that a piece of wood is straight and flat

Did You Know?

- More than 700,000 carpenters work in the United States.

- Carpenters build with metal as well as wood.

- Right angles are an important part of most carpentry work. (The corner of a square is a right angle.)

- Many schools hire carpenters to keep the buildings in good shape.

Want to Know More?

At the Library

Flanagan, Alice K., and Romie Flanagan (photographer). *Mr. Paul and Mr. Lueke Build Communities*. Danbury, Conn.: Children's Press, 1999.

Florian, Douglas. *A Carpenter*. New York: Greenwillow Books, 1991.

Leavitt, Jerome Edward, and Margrete Cunningham (illustrator). *Easy Carpentry Projects for Children*. New York: Dover Publications, 1986.

On the Web

Fine Woodworking Online

http://www.taunton.com/fw/

For an online magazine about working with wood

The Heartwood School for the Homebuilding Crafts

http://www.heartwoodschool.com/

To take an online tour of this renowned Massachusetts school

Through the Mail

Associated General Contractors of America

1957 E Street, N.W.

Washington, DC 20006

For general information on careers in the construction industry

On the Road

Hancock Shaker Village

Intersection of Highways 20 and 41

Pittsfield, MA 01201

413/443-0188

800/817-1137

http://www.hancockshakervillage.org/

To see carpenters make furniture in the Shaker tradition

Index

About the Author

Vicky Franchino has wanted to be a writer ever since she was a young girl and spent hours writing copy for fictional catalogs. As a freelance writer, she has worked for such varied groups as educational toy companies, greeting card companies, and universities. She holds a bachelor's degree from the University of Wisconsin in Madison. Vicky Franchino lives with her husband and their three daughters in Wisconsin.